www.tredition.de

AF186321

ulaila

no support but delight

www.tredition.de

© 2020 . Ulaila

Publisher:
tredition GmbH, Halenreie 40-44, 22359 Hamburg

ISBN
Paperback: 978-3-347-13627-4
Hardcover: 978-3-347-13628-1
e-Book: 978-3-347-13629-8

Lectorate: Nerine Buhlert

Cover Photo: Regina Hügli

Cover Design: Jorinde Boon

no support but delight

ulaila

for the lights,

immersed into

the darkness of the times

"und der weiche Schnee zerrinnt..."

on the ice-covered grass

of winter's end

i find the wren, dead,

its silky feathered tiny

body still warm.

my dry-frozen heart

shivers, starving

for tenderness.

now

i reach out
for you, my
heart is blown
apart. glass falls
into the container
in the backyard.
your breath on
my dry skin lets
me take flame
in the big fire, sleeping,
for eons, in the fibrous cells.
when this tinder blazes, i
feel that all the shards shall melt.

soothing snow

on the disheveled shrub

full of red berries:

blossoms gone,

sore flesh,

winter's feed for the birds.

the inner and the outer heart

keeping time with the rattling train
my heart wafts
in the flurrying snow. the snow
melts in my heart.

undrinkable

milk curdles in grained clouds
in black tea.
my thoughts have long
turned sour.
who will now
empty the cup?

tired, i force myself

into the sharp

edges of „i must",

hurting whatever

i touch. till tears

redeem the gnashing salt:

fatigue dissolves

into the day,

day lies on its back.

nothing to do.

comfort. a cup

nestles into

my hand, it

warms and softens

my chased life.

pssst, child, pssst...

i always call you

back, you can

rely on me.

take sip after

sip and watch

emptiness growing.

loyally the cup

nestles into my

hand is space.

in the grey wet dusk,

trees cloudy,

the light of the hazel

is blurry even with

eyes wide open. wind

screen wiper, branches

are waving: come.

the greenish light

rains into the dark earth.

what wants to stay is just

make-up. wake up.

the tulips have faded.

their transparent petals dance

in the heat above the radiator.

outside the window

snow adrift settles

on greening tips.

everything happens

later or sooner.

they have no

choice: the dry

petals fall

off their stems

in a whirl.

birds interweave

the wounds of space

with their song.

and the wind, always void,

can no longer be stopped

by any pain

in dancing for no reason

with birds on its fingertips.

late snow

time drizzles, dissolves
into warm earth:
nobody there who needs it.

bird shakes itself

after its bath and flies, the blue

sky has no end and no beginning.

songs spill over the firmament,

unseen stars in broad daylight.

but when the harsh

hand of the father

seizes the bird, the heart

draws in its neck.

the bony hand insists:

„tell me how to sing!"

don't you hear the stars?

nothing but silence

remains in the cage.

winter's end

the room receives me:
the graining of
the reliable chair,
the tentative shadow
of the lamp
and the tender curve
of the snow-drop
in the vase.
i am absorbed
by this warming womb.
the things are so happy:
they may be in expectancy.
and i am in peace
at last i am in peace.
no longer searching for food thanks to
this pulsing umbilical cord.

no support but delight

child

to wrap myself into your long hair,
so soft, nothing but scent remains.
with twirling curls
you wave after me
and disappear.
i find a shimmering
hair of yours
on my coat
and follow its curve.
nothing is straight any more.
everything is you.

sophie

there is nothing else to do in life

than to swing, day after day,

face dissolved into the blue skies,

the dancing curls are

drunken from the wind,

belly moves forward

and sinks back

in the flowered dress.

short legs in rubber boots

thrown into the air:

no support

but delight.

bicycle

child stares into the garden
with eyes wide open, becomes
large and sweeping,
drifting leaf in the wind,
blown headlong over the grass,
disappears into
the know-not-where.
touching her red bicycle
in the swaying
infinity.

rebecca

blond hair, millet gruel,

hand smaller than the spoon.

spoon? silvery dance

with the lips, the millet

nestles into

your mouth

and is at home.

when you eat, there is

no shortage and no

guilt. you eat,

and everybody

takes a seat.

mothers' line of eons

draws a deep, deep breath:

she's eating.

at last we are all satisfied.

your blond reflects

in the dark window,

first mother, ancestor.

never has the moon

been so very full.

joy

dizzy stillness in me.

shining points of grass are whirling

through veils of mist.

and then the flowering

is over. the petals

in my heart

let go, are blown away

by the wind

of the outbreath.

filling the air

with feeling, fresh.

the fragrance

nothing but a hunch.

i stay here,

naked, pollinated.

untouched river

the planning, the comparing

absorbed by poriferous cells.

cells, trembling foam,

burst into

a living nothing

in the calm.

diving through
the endless sea
of the organs. a wave
releases me
into the air, i glide
on a sea-gull's wing.
shivering in the sparkle
on water's plane,
a shrill scream
breaks out from me.

unheld,

the crackling plastic bag

puffs in the untouched river

and submerges to the forms

given by water.

do you really think it impossible

to fly while standing on the earth?

the day loves spending

you as a cloud,

a cirrus or a cumulus.

wind calms and rises.

your feet take you

wherever they want.

meadow

dandelions explode,
inner light of countless suns
retained for millions of years.
i am lost in the grass, a dense
forest from immemorial ages, pathless.
my heart is empty, funneling
the roar of infinity.

autumn of the i

this fish you told me about,

the one worth thousands of euros,

that is served with its heart

beating, costing the gourmet

his life if the cook fails:

this poisonous fish am i. i am the cook.

and eat must also i.

you are singing in the shower,

i walk under

an umbrella in the rain,

feet wet in the soaked shoes.

there is no difference, you say.

water everywhere.

washing up

the whole world sucked up
by this stinking sponge.
the dishes get clean,
piece by piece,
in the measure of «i must».
increasingly disgusting this
dish-broth with remains of food.
i drown myself in it:
"there you are, that's for
falling out of creation."
who gives the punishment?
a gentle turning of the collar-bone
and the obedient rolling of the head:
the plug shoots out of my neck
and i am empty and free.

electronic monitoring

please, free me
from this prison
at home, with ankle band
surveillance. the feet
belong to a stranger.
it lasts so long,
the time that i create
in my systematic assiduity.

to be a burning leaf,

blown by the autumn storm

to wherever you would want,

intoxicated with wild dancing.

why am i clinging

to the tree,

a junkie of gravity,

why can't i stop checking

whatsapp and the weather report

on my smart phone?

what keeps me in

this armor of time?

who creates the institution

for hopeless cases?

you remove my heart,

a shabby sofa, with a generous

grasp. i have no money

to replace it.

now also you've taken

the dusty lamp.

in the dark and empty space

between the lungs

there is no place

for me to sit.

i go astray in it:

where is the door?

i'm dizzy.

buzzing, unprotested

lets the walls wobble

and sucks me into

the hive as fodder

for the bees.

scorched, moist furniture

is thrown out of the window

of my burned out flat.

your door stays closed.

where can i settle now

without my photo albums,

with no passport?

my chased heart races, until

the red drop drowns

in the endless blue.

eat as long as you still have

a tongue and teeth.

it won't be long.

so briefly before

death, asks lalla,

are you enjoying your food?

there is no time to

toss and turn the

guilt in your mouth.

once the guilty one is eaten

no disgust remains for

saliva, juices, excrements.

the fork collects

whatever's on the plate.

no residue: here,

have this raspberry,

worm and all.

a bleep on the agenda

of the deceased:

appointment missed.

and no-one knows

the password to remove

the facebook-account.

my shoes stay put

until you wear them

and take them home.

funeral march for the i

it is not mine
it is not mine
it is just life. life.

i am not this
i am not this
i am the life. life.

it lives me as it likes
tralalala
and shoots the i to pieces,
pulls the tight stocking
over the head with a jerk,
letting the face bulk and soften.

and slowly does the blood
of the mine leak,
trickling into the dry earth. earth.
ah, beauty of dying:
instead of the trestle
the round, round earth. earth.

and living is
is dying is
is all that is. is.

i am not this
i am not this
i am this all. this.

when breath's liquid
crystal stagnates,
doubt jumps on me
from behind,
digging his claws
into my shoulder blades.
neck stiffens terrified
as a deep bite hollows
the heart. trust trickles out,
the lonely woman's blood
running down her stammering back.
poor heart, you have to wait
until the new moon's crescent
comes to fetch
the doubting trestle.

i let love's bomb belt

lay itself around my waist,

i feel the heat in kidneys, stomach.

wind through the heart

raises a smile on my face,

smile falters in

the metallic taste of fear.

there's no way back. the spark

of love jumps and ignites,

whenever you become i.

turned up

grass cut by the spade,
roots and all, is thrown
upside down into
a dark hole,
covered with earth.
nowhere from,
nowhere to.
no transformation.
i'm inside.

they have buried me.
mouth filled with soil,
the water of life
flows on in the maggots.
bones shimmering,
moonlight through trees.
it feels so good. and yet,
how i long for the kiss,
the sweet, sweet kiss!
when will the sun
rise again for me
and let the flowers sprout?

walking on the moon

at noon,

sun shivers

through the mist.

quite blurry,

everything is present.

my heartbeat pulses

near and afar.

a child calls.

waking up

in the grey morning
birds sing in the empty space.
every tone hurts, my heartbeat
ebbs away aswoon
through the hot limbs.
when i cannot sleep,
who is there then to wake up?
and if nobody wakes up,
who then needs sleep?

awake in the night

on my knees at half past three,
the terrace hard and cold,
face wet, long before the dew.
stars far away and blurred,
call of the owl
fades in my empty heart,
that can no longer pray.
the neighbor with his dog,
back from night-duty,
gazes over the hedge.
cat snuggles up
to my legs, is covering
my shame with tenderness.

echo of spring

when the shrubs and trees

jump out of their skin,

there is still a child

that wants to sleep.

when your oldest one

climbs into the highest tree tops,

searching for birds' nests,

there is still the little sister

crying for your breast.

when the birds

let the sky burst

with their singing, shouting,

there still is an old one

turning to the other side,

yearning for the dark.

o mother, keep me

immersed into your sweet sleep,

whether i am flower, seed, or soil.

sunrise

blinking: tears in the grass.
the sun explodes
out of the mountain lump.
earth, dazzled, sinks away
into dark blue.
birds sing.

the autumn sun spins

the juice back into the heart,

heart swirls under

the now fragile skin.

when the first storm comes,

skin will be torn, the body

rising as a flock of birds,

flying southward.

a breeze

gently caresses

what still is my face.

at last frost strikes

and makes an end

to the sluggish proliferation.

joy of the frozen

earth: nothing to do.

the greens yield faintly

on this mirror-smooth

edge of nothingness.

christmas tree

shimmering balls,
lights reflected.
a skeleton in the living room,
amidst the dancing cosmos.
the magic of this cheap
stuff is nothing
but gloss.
the needles trickle softly.

gentlest cave

no, i will not come for coffee

my friend, for the too sweet and dry

cake that makes me cough.

will not sit on that stiff chair,

on the cushion as if

it were my breath.

will have no talk that fixes things

in their frame and fixes

the frame itself. i will not enter

the hollow sounding armor

in our voices, in our sex,

a shell against the man, because

he is harder and faster than we.

come join me into the forest.

to be honest, i like

trees better than people,

but in their company

i enjoy being with you so much,

with our dancing breasts.

blue january

in the perfume of the moist green moss

i fall softly.

the wind in the dry grass

lets me smile.

when the bird takes wing

out of the heath,

freedom remains.

in the waning moon

the body turns night blue.

dotting the earth with countless stars,

buds singing in silence.

water is again aflow

in the creek bed.

the arid time forgotten

in the stream of lust.

at last i can

change my form

and all the

ferns, grasses and trees

join my dance.

the song of the birds

stirs sweetness now

in the heart,

lips shivering,

a kiss.

sigh. mind lays down

in the body. sun

breaks out of a blue hole

in the cloudy sky

and dances on the water.

fish glitter

and the waves

of my lake of lust

move gently between

the rolling hills of the pelvis.

flame burns between

the thighs, is cradled gently

by the breath.

soft the wax,

the wick relentless:

with smiling

irresistibility

my heart is cooked.

food for you.

is rose, is lily,

petals, chalice,

whirled up

in the breathing space,

until there is nothing but bloom,

without flowers, without sex.

nothing but fragrance.

warm wave passing

the sand of the hips

leaves the beach

with accurate drawing

at low tide.

tide burning

deletes all characters and letters

in the one heart.

between labor pangs

space fades away.

pain has its price,

the breathing body.

who is this?

they give me

the child: a

tiny bundle of freedom,

empty and silent.

substituted

one shot. torn
belly, my gaze
drawn downwards.
who cares
when i fall?
the red full moon
is sinking deep into
the endless sea.

sharing

to share you:
my bones shattered
by the force of the blow.
i can't call
on the marrow any more.
impossible to share
this pulp deprived of dignity.
nothing but red,
whimpering for
a shielding blue.

the earth: my pelvis

with its mountains, lakes and forests,

the rejoicing stars, the moon

softly shining on the waters,

and with you. you

walk through the valley,

your breath moving me

from the heart of the earth.

we hold each other so gently

in the warm house

of unspeakable love

trembling in the rough winds

with the walls.

you calm me, you say

there is enough wood for the fire,

to keep it burning night and day.

fire of our humanity, i say, that is

so exposed in the gales of love.

when you come

he calls you by no name

when you come

there is no talk.

nothing to explain

or to put right.

he knocks

he knocks

he knocks you

it knocks the knock

of infinity.

soundless scream,

when this

merciless lover

takes you.

in the bend

of this gentlest cave

your head is turned,

it dances, the eyes gaze

towards all sides.

your good right

gets crooked and laughs.

a miracle,

no special one.

and shouts.

when the body becomes desert,

fickle sand,

the dull tongue dry,

as if it never

kissed before,

the heart is strangled

by the carcass

of meaning.

press me, bones, until

i can't escape

my grief, let tears

moisten my lips,

go, press me

with futility.

tears fall

into my lap

and the hills

turn green again.

o fierce grief,

do not leave me

till all work is done

and the heart melts

in the dancing tongue,

kissed welcome home.

dawn

out of my warm blood
the sun rises
in the lighting blue
of my eyes.
from my perfume
flowers sprout
and through my breath
the wind soars,
flying leaves
whirl in my laughter
and in my moist cave
the forest awakens.
now that the body is earth,
the cosmos is me.

dahlias

round vase with short stems
on the table. in powerful
bright blossoms
the sound of your laughter
reverberates ahead
of the joke,
echoes in the silent room.
when leaves fall, you release
flower after flower,
exuberance of one
who hasn't much else to do.
ignition of beauty
in the misty garden, nothing
to lose, moist lipstick
amidst grey strands of hair,
your whole face a kiss.
hands black of soil,
digging out the tubers
before frost comes.
rest softly in
the basement, grandma,
in the shoe box.

dreamtime

the alder sings

the song of the place

where the seed fell, into

its fingertips, its toes. the brook,

shivering of lust,

glides into its meanders.

from deeper than

the brook, the tree:

heartbeat living us.

things are yet quite different.

watch through the eyes of the deer.

when the flesh

lets go of the bones,

the earth is round again.

when the flesh

lets go of the bones,

the cosmos is ripped open

and the moons shine.

when the flesh

lets go of the bones,

the waters flow

and my heart sings

flowers that sprout from me.

all seeds germinate

when the sower becomes sun.

hymn

o my gentle flame

that can burn

without a wick,

let the angular hips

roll with

the swinging legs,

don't let yourself be choked

by blue haze.

i don't need a man.

caressed by emptiness

in your middle,

i am ignited

by fleeting beauty.

my light, you cause

the living shadows,

brighten the dark earth

and take me with you

into the dance

of roots and toadstools.

o my joy

you flicker in

the golden leaves

and dissolve into

the bright blue sky.

nothing was ever there.

you dance.

even when the hardest of sounds

has ripped the organs of the whales,

when the oceans have turned red

and the widowed earth

is draped in grey desert,

even then will love give birth

to life anew through me:

my womb is sung into infinity

in this darkness

by the stars.

too busy living

quake in the heart: echo

of a sigh of relief

dissolves everything

that thinks to know itself

into pixels.

breath carries

the dancing swarm.

don't knock.

no one here.

too busy living.

presence floods

my brain.

water swells,

bright green

the cress within.

a silvery fish

darts through,

and the rowing green

is carried away

by the current.

bath

i am swimming and
my slippers dance
in the wind on the shore.
the fans of my feet, narrow
and hard from wanting,
spread into fins.
the water laughs. shouting:
the geese are back!

even softer my head, until

the skull plates, washed

by the oceans, move

over each other and apart

again. in a breeze

the skull bursts

in tenderness: blow

ball. seeds flying

through the air.

such brightness. it hurts.

truck

message on the radio:
truck has lost items
on the highway.
please drive carefully.
what is a truck
without a load?
what is life
without an object?
drive slowly...

"under-standing"

when my step is gracious
and easy, wanting nothing
but the ground,
the earth's womb
gives birth to me
into every life,
into yours, mine, or one in taiwan,
that of the nun, the farmer, of the wild woman,
hundreds, thousands, ten thousands of years ago.
i walk in their kitchen, bathroom,
by their hearth and well,
swallow the taste in their mouth
and feel their clothes on my skin.
lights, immersed into
the darkness of the times,
of the future or the past.
the earth infused
by a shining net.
my gaze dissolves
into twilight, a bright tremor
shakes my heart.
maybe this is
a fantasy,

but that doesn't matter:
we all are.
walk on, and let
the fragrance
of the moist soil flood you:
"under-standing", that
is being earth.

mandala

in earth's heart

all balls are in the air.

the absolute chaos

is harmony, in the heart.

the links between the molecules

stream asunder and

as the floor beneath my feet

dances me, the walls retract.

dying cat

for luna

when you
dissolve in space,
your honey eye a slit,
waning moon
melting into darkness,
your breath
a translucent thread –
the scrubby fur
is no longer needed.
so subtle the flesh,
that it is warmed
by the trembling
of the stars
in your belly.
when your body
becomes earth,
you float, a sphere
in blue space.
when everything remains,
where does then your name go?

Ulaila (Martina Hügli) is a poet, researcher of reality and gardener of life. Her first two books of poetry appeared under her civil name Martina Hügli in 1998 ("Nicht gegen uns selbst immun") and in 2000 ("am ohrenäquator", both in Axel Dielmann Verlag, Frankfurt a.M.), next to other poetic and essayistic publications and translations from Russian and American.

In 2002 a long writing pause began, led by the desire to return home into the poetry of reality beyond the written word. In 2016 a Dutch book appeared (Martina Hügli Boon, "Leven in wat je Doet", Free Musketeers), arising from 14 years of work in which Martina accompanied herself and other women into a slower and deeper life. Since 2015 she writes poetry again, which is collected in this book.

Martina Hügli, born in Switzerland, raised in England and Germany, lived in several European countries, in Russia and in the US. She is married, a mother of two daughters and a stepdaughter, and lives in a village in the South of the Netherlands.

You can find more information on

www.poetry-of-life.net

Zeitfracht Medien GmbH
Ferdinand-Jühlke-Straße 7
99095 Erfurt, Deutschland
produktsicherheit@kolibri360.de